ALABAMA

ALABAMA

HELLO
U.S.A.

by Dottie Brown

Lerner Publications Company

You'll find this picture of a cotton field at the beginning of each chapter in this book. Cotton is one of Alabama's most important crops. Farmers gather and sell the fibers of the cotton plant, which grows in a pod called a boll. People all over the world wear clothing made from cotton fibers picked in Alabama.

Cover (left): The USS *Alabama* in its moorings at the USS *Alabama* Battleship Memorial Park in Mobile. Cover (right): Cotton plant, Monroe County. Pages 2–3: Moundville Archaeological Park, Moundville. Page 3: Flower garden at Linn Park, Birmingham.

This book is available in two editions:
Library binding by Lerner Publications Company, a division of Lerner Publishing Group
Soft cover by First Avenue Editions, an imprint of Lerner Publishing Group
241 First Avenue North
Minneapolis, MN 55401 U.S.A.

Website address: www.lernerbooks.com

Library of Congress Cataloging-in-Publication Data

Brown, Dottie, 1957–
    Alabama / by Dottie Brown. (Rev. and expanded 2nd ed.)
      p.   cm. — (Hello U.S.A.)
    Includes index.
    Summary: Introduces the geography, history, economy, famous people, and environment of the Heart of Dixie.
      ISBN: 0–8225–4067–3 (lib. bdg. : alk. paper)
      ISBN: 0–8225–4143–2 (pbk. : alk. paper)
      1. Alabama—Juvenile literature. [1. Alabama.] I. Title. II. Series.
    F326.3.B76 2002
    976.1—dc21   2001002960

Manufactured in the United States of America
1 2 3 4 5 6 – JR – 07 06 05 04 03 02

CONTENTS

An early morning illuminates the peaceful land of the Heart of Dixie.

THE LAND

The Heart of Dixie

he word *Dixie* is sometimes used to describe the South, a region that covers the southeastern section of the United States. Alabama, located near the center of the region, is known as the Heart of Dixie.

Alabama is bordered by four other states. Mississippi lies in the west, and Georgia is to the east. North of Alabama is Tennessee, and Florida sits to the south. The Gulf of Mexico, part of the Atlantic Ocean, washes against the southwestern tip of Alabama.

Rivers flow throughout much of Alabama. The state's longest rivers are the Alabama and the Tombigbee. These waterways meet in southwestern Alabama and form the Mobile River, which flows through Mobile Bay into the Gulf. Other chief rivers include the Tennessee and the Chattahoochee.

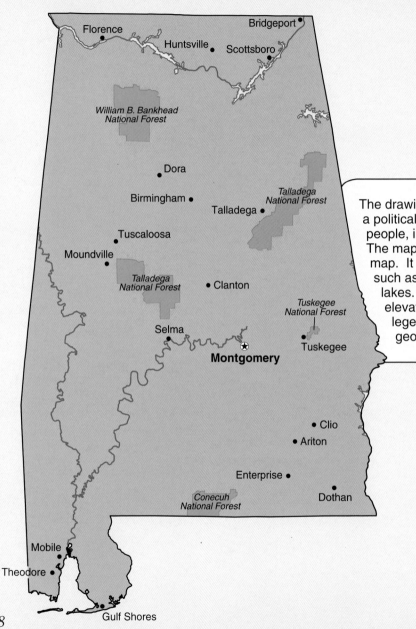

Florence

Bridgeport

Huntsville
Scottsboro

William B. Bankhead
National Forest

Dora

Birmingham

Talladega
National Forest

Talladega

Tuscaloosa

Moundville

Talladega
National Forest

Clanton

Tuskegee
National Forest

Selma

Montgomery

Tuskegee

Clio

Ariton

Enterprise

Conecuh
National Forest

Dothan

Mobile

Theodore

Gulf Shores

N
W   E
S

The drawing of Alabama on this page is called a political map. It shows features created by people, including cities, railways, and parks. The map on the facing page is called a physical map. It shows physical features of Alabama, such as coasts, islands, mountains, rivers, and lakes. The colors represent a range of elevations, or heights above sea level (see legend box). This map also shows the geographical regions of Alabama.

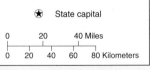

ALABAMA
Political Map

★   State capital

0   20   40 Miles

0   20   40   60   80 Kilometers

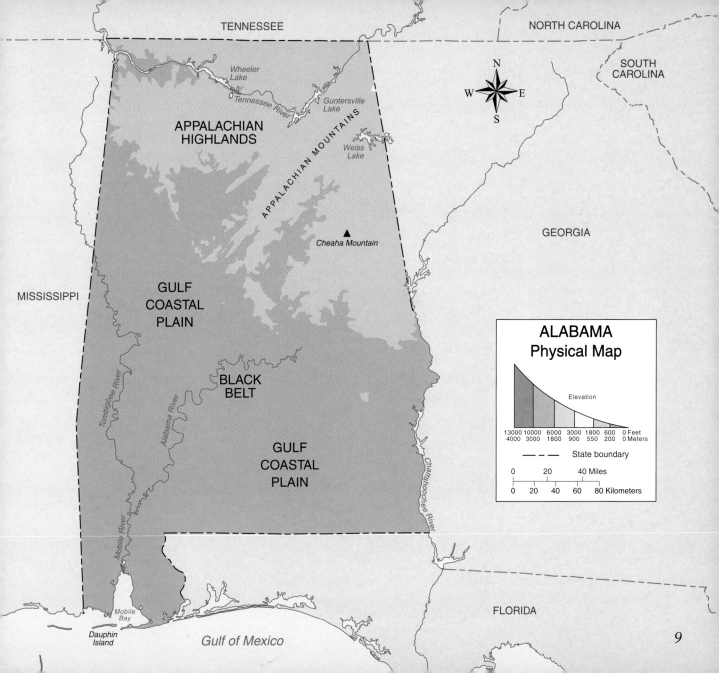

TENNESSEE

NORTH CAROLINA

SOUTH CAROLINA

Wheeler Lake

Tennessee River

Guntersville Lake

APPALACHIAN HIGHLANDS

Weiss Lake

APPALACHIAN MOUNTAINS

GEORGIA

▲
Cheaha Mountain

MISSISSIPPI

GULF COASTAL PLAIN

Tombigbee River

Alabama River

BLACK BELT

GULF COASTAL PLAIN

Chattahoochee River

Mobile River

Mobile Bay

Dauphin Island

FLORIDA

Gulf of Mexico

N
W E
S

ALABAMA
Physical Map

Elevation

13000	10000	6000	3000	1800	600	0 Feet
4000	3000	1800	900	550	200	0 Meters

– – – State boundary

0	20	40 Miles

0	20	40	60	80 Kilometers

9

Locks—water-filled chambers that allow boats to pass waterfalls—have been built along some of Alabama's rivers. Huge dams on these waterways control water depth to help prevent flooding. The dams hold back extra water after heavy rains, forming **reservoirs,** or artificial lakes. The lake water is then slowly released to power engines that produce electricity.

At the Miller Ferry dam on the Alabama River, water from a reservoir rushes through opened gates. The flowing water powers engines that generate electricity.

The reservoirs also supply water to nearby cities and towns. Alabama's largest lakes are actually reservoirs. The biggest are Guntersville, Wheeler, and Weiss.

Lakes and rivers are found in all of Alabama's three land regions—the Appalachian Highlands, the Gulf Coastal Plain, and the Black Belt. The landscapes of these regions vary from flat, sandy beaches to low, pine-covered mountains.

Hikers enjoy the view from Cheaha, Alabama's highest point. The mountain peak rises 2,407 feet above sea level.

The Gulf of Mexico washes the shores of Dauphin Island, part of Alabama's Gulf Coastal Plain.

The Appalachian Highlands region is situated in the northeastern part of the state. This area contains the southern end of the Appalachian Mountains, the oldest mountain system in North America. Minerals such as coal, iron ore, and limestone lie beneath many of the highlands' ridges and valleys. Birmingham, Alabama's largest city, sits on top of some of these deposits.

Alabama's largest land region, the Gulf Coastal Plain, covers nearly two-thirds of the state. Low, rolling hills blanket the northern half of the plain. **Swamps,** or wetlands, fill the flat southwestern section of the region. Soil along much of the western edge of the plain is too rocky and sandy to farm, but the rich soil in the eastern area is suitable for many crops.

The Black Belt is a strip of gently rolling land that slices through the middle of the Gulf Coastal Plain. The fertile black soil of the belt is some of Alabama's

Wildflowers overflow a field in springtime.

best farmland. At one time, cotton **plantations** (large farms) sprawled across the region. In modern times, many farmers raise livestock and grow vegetables and other crops in the Black Belt.

A long growing season benefits Alabama's farmers. The state's weather is generally mild in the winter and hot in the summer. During the winter, northern Alabama is slightly colder than the southern half of the state. The average winter temperature throughout Alabama is a warm 50° F. Summer temperatures tend to be about the same all over the state, averaging around 80° F.

An electrical storm in western Alabama

Alabama is a well-watered land. An average of 59 inches of **precipitation** (rain, snow, sleet, and hail) falls each year in the state, mostly as rain. Northern Alabama gets a few light snowfalls in winter.

Tornadoes and hurricanes occasionally blast through the state. These fierce storms can yank up trees, rip apart homes, and mangle docks. Most of the time, however, Alabama's weather is tame.

Forests of pine, cedar, cypress, hemlock, and oak blanket about two-thirds of Alabama. Spanish moss, a plant that grows without roots, drapes itself over tree limbs. Many fragrant, flowering trees and shrubs such as magnolias, dogwoods, mountain laurels, and azaleas perfume the air. Orchids, asters, goldenrods, and other flowering plants add their beauty to the forests.

Wooded areas are home to much of Alabama's wildlife. Bobcats stalk rabbits in the state's tree-covered mountains. Red foxes and gray foxes prowl through dense stands of trees, where opossums, mink, and skunks scurry about. Alligators slither through Alabama's southern swamps, and beavers gnaw saplings, which the animals use to build their homes in the state's lowlands.

Red foxes make their homes in Alabama's forests.

Marching Forward

The glow of a blazing fire cast dancing shadows inside a huge cave in northeastern Alabama. It was a chilly winter evening, and the hunters in the cave warmed themselves around the fire while supper roasted. An artist among them painted pictures on the cave's walls.

People who later found these paintings realized that the cave's inhabitants weren't just ordinary campers. Scientists examined the hunting and cooking tools left behind and determined that the hunters most likely lived about 8,000 years ago. They were probably Alabama's first people.

Traces of other early peoples exist throughout the state. Burial mounds heaped up about 800 years ago by Indians known as mound builders still stand

Hundreds of years ago, Native Americans created the burial mounds that rise in Mound State Monument in Moundville, Alabama.

in southeastern Alabama. The mound-building Indians lived in villages and planted corn. They traveled far to trade pottery and jewelry for copper and seashells with other Indians.

Some experts believe that mound builders are the ancestors of the Choctaw, Chickasaw, and Creek Indians. Members of these Native American nations hunted and fished in Alabama. They were also farmers who grew corn, beans, squash, and melons. The Indians of these nations shared some customs and spoke a similar language, called Muskogean.

Hernando de Soto

Indians were living in Alabama for hundreds of years before Spanish explorer Hernando de Soto arrived in 1540. De Soto, the first European to explore the region, marched a band of 950 soldiers into Choctaw territory to look for gold. A group of Choctaw Indians, who considered the armed Spaniards to be intruders, barred their way. But the Spaniards broke through, killed the Indians, and burned their village.

A few other Spaniards visited the region after de Soto, but the French were the first to establish a permanent European settlement there. In 1702 two French-Canadian brothers, Pierre and Jean Baptiste Le Moyne, founded Fort Louis de la Mobile on a bluff near the Mobile River.

Because of flooding, in 1711 the fort was moved farther south to the site of what later became Mobile. In 1720 the fort was renamed Fort Condé. In 1763, at the end of the French and Indian War, the French lost Fort Condé and most of their other

North American holdings to the British and the Spaniards. As a result, Britain claimed almost all the land between the Mississippi River and the Atlantic Ocean, including Alabama.

Along the Atlantic coast, Britain had divided its territory into **colonies.** In 1775, to gain their independence, 13 of the colonies started fighting Britain in a war that became known as the American Revolution. Britain lost the war in 1783, and the 13 former colonies formed a new country—the United States of America.

Between 1702 and 1722, Fort Louis de la Mobile was capital of France's Louisiana Territory.

Tecumseh Puts His Foot Down

Tecumseh (1768?–1813) was a Shawnee Indian leader. He was a skilled warrior and a gifted speaker. He traveled across the country working to unite all Indians against the invasion of white American settlers.

Tecumseh lived for a time in Detroit, Michigan. In 1811 he traveled to the Creek village of Tuckabatchee in Alabama. Indians there refused to join Tecumseh in his plans for war, a reaction that angered the leader. According to one story, Tecumseh said, "When I get back to Detroit, I will stamp my foot upon the ground and shake every house in Tuckabatchee."

One month later—about the time Tecumseh reached Detroit—a powerful earthquake shook parts of Alabama. The Indians of Tuckabatchee ran from their homes shouting, "Tecumseh has reached Detroit! We feel the shake of his foot!"

European settlers raised tobacco and other crops on Alabama's farmland.

Britain had lost more than the colonies in the American Revolution. It also had to give much of its land in North America to Spain, which had assisted the colonists by declaring war on the British. Spain then agreed to give some territory, including most of Alabama, to the United States.

People from the United States began moving into Alabama looking for fertile farmland. Many newcomers settled on the Indians' territory. Besides the Choctaw, Chickasaw, and Creek, the Cherokee Indians made new homes in Alabama. These nations tried to get along with the settlers, adopting European customs. But they could not allow the newcomers to keep taking Indian land.

In 1813, angry about losing their land, a group of Indians known as the Red Stick Creek attacked Fort Mims, a pioneer settlement on the Alabama River. The Indians killed hundreds of men, women, and children.

A band of Creek called the White Stick joined the Chickasaw, Choctaw, and Cherokee Indians in fighting what became known as the Creek War. In 1814

Pioneers at Fort Mims didn't expect an attack by the Red Stick Creek Indians. In this image, the artist depicts the pioneers as helpless.

these Indians and U.S. troops, led by General Andrew Jackson, won the Battle of Horseshoe Bend against the Red Stick Creek. Afterward, the general insisted that all Creek—including the White Stick—give up their land, which covered about half of Alabama. The Creek had to move to a small area in eastern Alabama.

The Creek War opened up land to U.S. settlers, who began to pour into Alabama. They came from Virginia, Georgia, Tennessee, and beyond. Some of Alabama's new settlers were blacksmiths, machinists, and wagon makers who had come to fight in the Creek War and had decided to stay. All were looking for a better life and fertile land. By 1819 Alabama had a large enough population to become the 22nd state of the United States.

Most Alabamians owned small plots of land, which they farmed themselves. But some planters used black people who had been brought by force from Africa to work as slaves. The slave-owning planters earned the most money for Alabama from producing cotton.

Plantation slaves had to work long hours and carry heavy loads of cotton.

Cotton was grown mainly to make clothing. The crop was so important to the state's economy that the fluffy white crop was called "King Cotton."

The planters grew their cotton in the fertile soil of Alabama's Black Belt. The dirt was rich in the nutrients needed to grow healthy crops, but the land was hard to plow. Planters depended on slaves to do the difficult jobs of plowing the fields and handpicking the cotton at harvesttime.

The cotton gin saved planters time and money. The invention removed seeds from cotton much faster than people could.

Montgomery, on the edge of the Black Belt, was the town where buyers and sellers of cotton bargained for the best prices. It became a center of activity—a prosperous town where doctors, lawyers, merchants, and bankers built elegant mansions.

By the mid-1800s, about one-third of Alabamians owned slaves. Nearly everyone in the state depended in one way or another on plantations worked by slaves. Some purchased the cotton from planters and then sold it to clothing manufacturers for a profit. Others simply bought and wore the clothing made from Alabama's cotton.

Southern leaders met in Montgomery to choose a president of the Confederate States of America. They selected Jefferson Davis.

While the South relied on slave labor, the North, with its factories and smaller farms, did not. Many Northerners believed slavery was wrong and tried to persuade the U.S. government to make slavery illegal in all states.

Southern plantation owners argued that they would go broke if they had to give up slaves. Southerners also believed strongly in the right to make their own decisions and disliked Northerners meddling in Southern affairs.

Abraham Lincoln, a Northerner, was elected president of the United Sates in 1860. Fearing that slavery would become illegal across the country,

Alabama withdrew from the United States early in 1861. Several other Southern states joined Alabama and organized the Confederate States of America, a new country where slavery was legal. Shortly afterward the Civil War broke out between the North (the Union) and the South (the Confederacy).

At least 120,000 Alabamians fought for the Confederacy. The most important Civil War battle in Alabama took place at Mobile Bay in 1864. Union troops captured Mobile Bay and prevented the port from sending or receiving supplies.

The Union navy blocked Mobile's port after the Battle of Mobile Bay. The effort weakened Confederate forces in Alabama.

The Union won the war in 1865, and all Confederate slaves were freed. After four long years of war, parts of Alabama were in shambles. Food and money were scarce. Union troops had looted and torched several towns, had destroyed crops, and had stolen livestock.

After the Civil War, during a period known as **Reconstruction,** Northern lawmakers and businesspeople ran Alabama's government. They oversaw the building of new roads and made sure black men were given the right to vote. But many of the Northerners did more harm than good. Called **carpetbaggers** by Southerners, the dishonest or inexperienced Northerners stole or wasted government money, hurting the economy they were supposed to be helping.

During Reconstruction, Alabamians set out to rebuild their state. Farmers readied the soil for planting cotton. With its rich supply of minerals, Birmingham began producing large amounts of iron and steel. Workers laid railroad tracks so trains could carry the iron and steel to Northern markets.

Students at the Tuskegee Normal and Industrial Institute conduct experiments in a science laboratory.

A School of Their Own

After the Civil War, black Americans set out to carve a new place for themselves in society. They wanted to farm their own land and run their own businesses. Laws in the South prevented African Americans from attending white schools, so they opened schools of their own.

In 1881 a former slave named Booker T. Washington founded a school in Tuskegee, Alabama, for African Americans. Called the Tuskegee Normal and Industrial Institute, the school taught practical skills, giving black men and women a chance to find work and make money. Many graduates became farmers, teachers, and mechanics.

The school later changed its name to Tuskegee University and began offering bachelor's and master's degrees. The nearly 3,000 African American students at the university major in dozens of fields, including business, engineering, architecture, nursing, and veterinary medicine.

By the 1890s, cloth and lumber companies also had grown, providing jobs and money for the state.

The United States entered World War I in 1917, further boosting Alabama's economy. Shipbuilders in Mobile manufactured battleships, while farmers in the state grew food for soldiers. Workers at textile mills used Alabama's cotton to make military uniforms.

Large crews worked to cut down timber in the late 1800s. Workers used the lumber to construct new buildings in Alabama and elsewhere in the South.

Many Alabama families lived in poverty during the Great Depression.

After the war, Alabama built highways and began making many new products, including copper wire, paper, tires, and freight cars. But people in the United States soon felt the effects of the Great Depression, a nationwide period of economic hardship that lasted throughout the 1930s. Banks and other businesses across the nation closed down. Many people lost their jobs and their savings.

Relief came when then President Franklin D. Roosevelt created thousands of new jobs nationwide through a program called the New Deal. For Alabama, one of the most important parts of the New Deal was the Tennessee Valley Authority (TVA), an organization formed in 1933. The TVA put hundreds of Alabamians to work building dams to control seasonal flooding on the Tennessee River and to generate electricity.

The electricity provided by the dams was inexpensive. Some companies moved to Alabama because cheap electric power would help keep business costs down. In addition, many homeowners in Alabama received electricity for the first time, allowing them to use modern conveniences such as lightbulbs and radios.

But the dams and reservoirs also permanently flooded acres and acres of land, forcing many people to abandon homes their families had owned for generations. Many of these Alabamians were against the TVA.

During World War II (1939–1945), TVA dams powered plants in northern Alabama where missiles,

rockets, and other military equipment were produced. After the war, a team of scientists came to one of these plants, the Redstone Arsenal in Huntsville, and developed the nation's first earth satellite. The satellite gathered information about space and about the planet Earth.

During World War II, Alabamians built the *Cayuse 269* for the U.S. Navy.

Rosa Parks Says No

On her way home from work one day in 1955, a woman named Rosa Parks *(above, right)*, from Montgomery, sat on a seat in the middle of a city bus. After all the seats in the front of the bus were taken, the driver ordered Parks to give up her seat for another passenger and to move to the rear. Parks refused and was arrested.

Parks, an African American, was asked to move so a white person could have her seat. A law enforced throughout the South stated that black people had to sit at the back of buses.

Rosa Parks's arrest outraged a young black minister in Montgomery named Martin Luther King Jr. He immediately organized a peaceful protest. African Americans refused to ride the city's buses for more than a year. The protest ended in 1956 when the U.S. Supreme Court ruled that all bus riders—regardless of race—could sit wherever they wanted.

While technology advanced, African Americans throughout the country were held back. Many were denied jobs because of their color. Black people did not have the same rights as white people. In Alabama and other southern states, laws called Jim Crow laws prevented blacks from using the same drinking fountains, hospitals, elevators, and cemeteries as whites. The black **civil rights movement** began in response to these unfair laws.

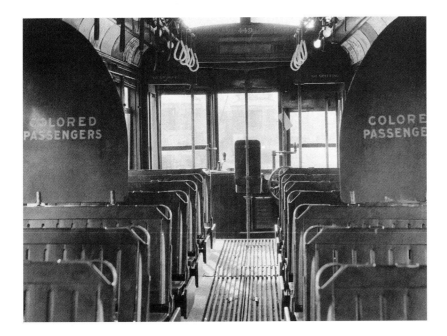

In public places throughout the south, laws separated black people and white people. The laws were in effect from the 1880s until the 1960s.

On their way from Selma to Montgomery, protesters walked across the Edmund Pettus Bridge.

In 1954 the U.S. Supreme Court ruled that it was illegal to have separate public schools for black students and white students. By 1963 African Americans had not been admitted to any state-run universities in Alabama. That year a judge ordered the University of Alabama to allow two black students to enroll.

African Americans all over the country were treated unfairly in other ways as well. Although black men and women had the right to vote in the United States, many cities found ways to get around the law. These places required African Americans to pay a tax they couldn't afford or to take a test that many couldn't pass.

Governor George C. Wallace

George C. Wallace, born in Clio, Alabama, was first elected governor of the state in 1962, during the civil rights movement. The next year, Wallace showed the nation his position on civil rights by standing in the doorway to try and block two black students from entering the University of Alabama for the first time. But he could not change the law, and by the mid-1960s, many of Alabama's schools were attended by both black and white students.

Throughout his political career, Wallace insisted that he did not dislike black people but felt that both races would be better off if kept separate. His major complaint against civil rights laws was that they were set by the U.S. government. Wallace strongly believed in the right of each state to have control over its own affairs.

During the 1960s and 1970s, Wallace ran unsuccessfully for president of the United States. While campaigning in Maryland in 1972, he was shot five times. The incident left his legs paralyzed. He was elected to Alabama's governorship again in 1970, 1974, and 1982.

Wallace had always promised to help all needy Alabamians. During his last campaign for governor, his views on civil rights changed somewhat. He no longer wanted to keep blacks and white separate and won the support of many black voters. Wallace died in 1998.

...UNTIL JUSTICE ROLLS DOWN LIKE WATERS AND RIGHTEOUSNESS LIKE A MIGHTY STREAM

MARTIN LUTHER KING JR

A memorial honors people who died in the civil rights movement. Built in 1989, the memorial stands outside the Southern Poverty Law Center in Montgomery.

By 1965 the city of Selma, Alabama, still had not allowed most African American residents to register to vote. In protest, Martin Luther King Jr. helped organize what started out as a peaceful march from Selma to Montgomery, the state capital.

Before they could even reach Montgomery, the protesters were stopped and beaten by state troopers. The day is remembered as "Bloody Sunday." The marchers, however, did not give up. King scheduled another protest, leading 25,000 people to the steps of Montgomery's capitol building. Shortly afterward, the U.S. government outlawed the tough requirements used by southern states to keep black people from voting.

African Americans in Alabama began voting for politicians they felt would speak for them. Over the years, blacks have been elected to serve as mayors and city council members throughout the state. In 1989 the people of Alabama created a civil rights memorial in Montgomery. In 2000 voters repealed a part of the state constitution that banned the marriage of black and white Alabamians. In 1967 the U.S. Supreme Court had ruled that such bans cannot be enforced. Even so, the people of Alabama wanted to remove the reminder of the days before the civil rights movement.

Both black and white Alabamians, as well as other Americans, still work to get along. Many Alabamians realize that the best future for their state is in providing the same opportunities to all its citizens.

To ensure that Alabamians have good jobs, Alabama has been working to attract new companies to the state. Alabama is among the south's leading producers of high-tech products, from medicine to rockets.

Service First

In 1919 the people of Enterprise erected a statue dedicated to the boll weevil.

Enterprise, Alabama, may be the only city in the world with a statue honoring an insect. The town's citizens put up the monument to thank boll weevils for destroying most of the area's cotton crops in the early 1900s.

Why would a town do that? For many years, King Cotton determined how much money the people of Enterprise and other farming areas in Alabama made. When the cotton harvest was small or sold for low prices, everyone suffered. After the boll weevil invaded Alabama, farmers were forced to raise livestock and to plant crops that the beetle

To harvest cotton, Alabamians operate machines called pickers. The machine pulls the cotton from the plant and then blows the fiber into a large metal storage compartment.

wouldn't attack. The farmers ended up making even more money than they had from cotton.

Alabama is still a leading cotton-growing state, and cotton is Alabama's primary crop. Alabama's farmers also grow corn, hay, oats, wheat, peanuts, pecans, and timber. Three-fourths of the money made from the state's farms is earned from livestock such as chickens, cattle, and hogs. Beekeepers raise bees for their honey and wax. Altogether, farmers make up 4 percent of the state's workers.

Alabama's biggest moneymaker is services—that is, jobs where workers help other people or businesses. About 56 percent of the state's jobholders are service workers. Among them are salespeople, doctors, waitpeople, bankers, auto mechanics, and tour guides. Government workers make up about 16 percent of Alabama's workforce. Soldiers stationed at military bases in the state fly jets, repair machinery, and direct air traffic. At the government-run George C. Marshall Space Flight Center, scientists design rockets.

A farmer will milk these dairy cows. Alabama's farmers profit most from the sales of livestock products, which include milk.

Manufacturing employs 17 percent of Alabama's workforce. Laborers in the state's pulp and paper industry operate mills that process wood into paper, cardboard, and tissue. These products are treated with chemicals prepared in the state. Workers in the state's chemical plants also mix fertilizers and produce artificial fibers needed to make certain types of cloth.

These logs will be processed at a lumber mill.

Offshore oil wells dot the Gulf of Mexico near Alabama.

Alabama ranks 15th in the nation in coal production. Thousands of the state's miners—1 percent of Alabama's workers—operate machines to dig for coal or to drill for oil and natural gas. Others scoop limestone out of the earth's surface for use in making steel and cement. Alabama's minerals and manufactured products are shipped to other states and countries from Mobile, one of the busiest ports in the nation.

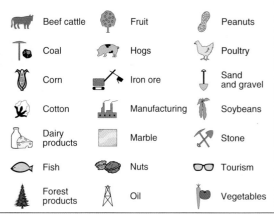

ALABAMA
Economic Map

The symbols on this map show where different economic activities take place in Alabama. The legend below explains what each symbol stands for.

Symbol		Symbol		Symbol	
	Beef cattle		Fruit		Peanuts
	Coal		Hogs		Poultry
	Corn		Iron ore		Sand and gravel
	Cotton		Manufacturing		Soybeans
	Dairy products		Marble		Stone
	Fish		Nuts		Tourism
	Forest products		Oil		Vegetables

45

A Native American man plays his flute at a Moundville, Alabama, festival.

With more than 4 million people calling Alabama home, the 22nd state to join the Union ranks 23rd in the nation in population. About three out of every five Alabamians live in cities. The largest of these are Birmingham, Montgomery (the state capital), Mobile, and Huntsville.

Most of Alabama's residents have English, French, or Spanish ancestors. One-fourth of the state's population is African American. Although several Indian nations once lived throughout the area, fewer than 8,000 Creek and Choctaw remain in Alabama.

Whatever their background, Alabamians have a rich history. Artifacts at the Indian Mound and Museum in Florence reveal the story of the state's mound-building Indians. At Fort Condé in Mobile, tour guides dressed in soldiers' uniforms tell stories about what life was like at the fort in the early 1700s. Visitors to Tuskegee can tour the George Washington Carver Museum. Exhibits there show the accomplishments of George Washington Carver, who studied plants and was one of the most famous instructors at Tuskegee Institute.

Tours at Fort Condé in Mobile are a popular tourist attraction.

Paintings and sculptures draw crowds at the Birmingham Museum of Art. The Montgomery Museum of Fine Arts houses paintings by southern artists and a special hands-on gallery for children. Music lovers can relax and enjoy symphony orchestras in Birmingham, Mobile, Huntsville, and

Aboard the USS *Alabama,* tourists can see the heavy artillery and workings of a real battleship.

Rocket Park, part of the U.S. Space and Rocket Center, displays a lunar module. The spacecraft was used to land astronauts on the moon.

Tuscaloosa. A stop in Florence will bring you to a childhood home of W. C. Handy, a musician known as the Father of the Blues.

Alabama is one of the few places in the country where folks can board a real battleship, the USS *Alabama*, anchored in Mobile Bay. Huntsville is home to the largest space museum in the world— the U.S. Space and Rocket Center.

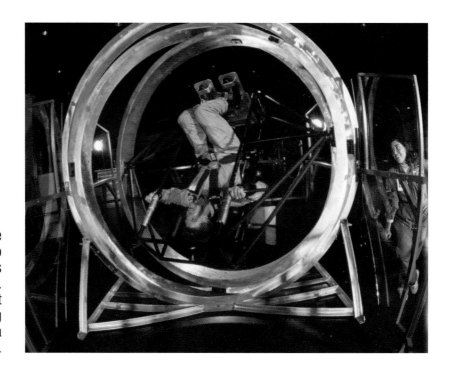

Students come to the U.S. Space Camp to experience what it is like to be an astronaut. Here, a student experiences the feeling of space from a multi-axis gyro.

Visitors to Huntsville's space center can learn how it feels to walk in outer space, can examine rockets close-up, and can experience Mars Mission—a ride that makes you feel that you've been to the planet. The U.S. Space Camp, which is part of the center, teaches young students about careers in space.

Alabama offers a lot to sports enthusiasts. Hikers wander through giant caves at Carlsbad and

Sequoyah Caverns. Campers sleep under the stars in Conecuh, one of four national forests in Alabama. Boaters ride and fish in Alabama's lakes and in the Gulf of Mexico. Racing fans can watch greyhounds run in Tuskegee or stock cars speed around the track at Talladega.

Each fall, people flock to the University of Alabama to cheer the Crimson Tide, one of the best college football teams in the country. Excitement runs high when the Crimson Tide play their Alabama rival—the Tigers of Auburn University.

Thousands of fans cheer on the Crimson Tide football team.

The Birmingham Barons, a minor league baseball team, entertain Alabamians with one of America's best-loved sports.

Whether wanting to relax, have fun, or catch a glimpse of bygone days, people can find plenty to enjoy in Alabama—the Heart of Dixie.

Sailors navigate the Gulf of Mexico.

THE ENVIRONMENT

Treasuring Forests

 orests cover about two-thirds of Alabama and are one of the state's most important natural resources. Mobile is the nation's number-one-ranked exporter of wood pulp and the second-ranked exporter of forest products. In addition to supplying timber, woodlands hold soil in place and provide homes for wildlife. Forests also serve as recreational areas and help make Alabama a beautiful place to live.

Trucks transport harvested logs.

Hiking trails wind through Alabama's scenic forested parkland.

Some of Alabama's forests are run by the state or the U.S. government. These areas are meant to be enjoyed by all. Most of the state's forestland is owned and run by private individuals or companies. Much of Alabama's privately owned forestland is healthy, but some landowners unknowingly allow their forests' natural cycle of growth and decay to be disrupted.

Some forest owners, for example, allow logging companies to cut down areas of forest without planning to create a new forest. While this practice gives new plants a chance to grow, creating homes for some animals, it also disturbs the habitat of other animals. And with no trees to hold soil in place, the soil may erode, or be washed away by rain.

To encourage landowners to take care of their forests, the Alabama Forestry Planning Committee developed the TREASURE Forest program in 1974. The letters in TREASURE stand for some important elements of a forest—Timber, Recreation, Environment, Aesthetics (beauty), Sustained, Usable, and REsource.

Black bears and other wildlife thrive in Alabama's forests.

The TREASURE program encourages private owners to get more than just timber out of their forestland. Landowners who participate in this program decide on two or more main uses for their land. They can choose timber, wildlife, recreation, natural beauty, or environmental education. They also must agree to protect their forests from erosion, from water pollution, and from wildfires. Forests that meet the program's goals become TREASURE Forests.

TREASURE Forest landowners who manage their forests mainly for timber may need to thin out overcrowded stands of trees. When trees grow too close together, none of them grow very big. The larger the tree, the more money it will bring when sold for timber.

Forest managers may even set fire to a small area

Seedlings grow in a forest area that has been recently burned. Controlled fires set by forest managers can help longleaf pines thrive.

of forest to encourage the growth of a particular tree, such as the longleaf pine. Longleaf pines, which are ideal for lumber and pulp, can survive fires that kill other trees. Once the other trees are burned, sunshine and bare soil allow longleaf pine seedlings to take root and thrive.

Managing a forest for timber also means growing new trees after harvesting to ensure a timber supply for the future. Alabamians plant more trees than they harvest.

Forest managers burn undergrowth to allow light to reach the ground. Grass then carpets the forest floor, providing pasture for livestock.

Landowners who manage their forests for wildlife can increase the number and kinds of wild animals living there. Knowing that some animals need young forests and other animals need old forests, these landowners choose to raise a variety of trees in different states of growth. These efforts have helped Alabama's animal population increase dramatically.

Nearly 1,500 Alabamians participate in the TREASURE Forest program. But that covers only about 12.5 percent of the state's forests. Some landowners don't join the program because they think the changes will cost too much and will take too much effort.

Young people interested in forestry can get involved in the Junior TREASURE Forest program. Under this program, they thin stands of trees, plant new trees, and work on projects that help prevent soil erosion. Young and old people alike are working to make sure Alabama's forests have a healthy future.

Alabama's people and its wildlife can enjoy well-maintained TREASURE Forests.

ALL ABOUT ALABAMA

Fun Facts

Scientists at the Marshall Space Flight Center in Huntsville, Alabama, developed the spacecraft that thrust U.S. astronauts all the way to the moon.

During the Civil War, Montgomery became the first capital of the Confederacy. For this reason, Montgomery is still called the Cradle of the Confederacy.

In 1955 Martin Luther King Jr., a minister, started the black civil rights movement at the Dexter Avenue Baptist Church in Montgomery, Alabama. King's non-violent protests led to fairer treatment for African Americans.

Dexter Avenue Baptist Church

The U.S. Army Aviation Museum at Fort Rucker houses more than 100 helicopters, making it one of the largest collections of choppers in the nation.

Alabama once almost split into two states. Just before the Civil War began in 1861, northern Alabamians came close to forming a new state called Nick-a-Jack. The founders of Nick-a-Jack did not want to withdraw from the United States, as Alabama had done.

Alabama is the only state in the United States with all the basic natural resources needed to produce iron and steel. Coal and limestone, two main minerals used in making iron and steel, are found close together throughout northern Alabama.

Alabama takes its name from the Alibamu, an Indian group that once lived in the region. Alibamu means, "I clear the thicket."

STATE SONG

Alabama's state song was adopted in 1931.

ALABAMA

Music by Edna Gockel Gussen
Lyrics by Julia S. Tutwiler

You can hear "Alabama" by visiting this website:
<http://www.50states.com/songs/alabama.htm>

AN ALABAMA RECIPE

Okra is the main ingredient in
gumbo—the well-known southern
soup. But it's also great in salads or
fried. Okra was brought to the southern
United States by African slaves generations ago. Try the
simple recipe below to find out why okra is healthy and delicious.

FRIED OKRA

⅓ cup plain flour
⅓ cup cornmeal (white)
1 teaspoon salt
1½ pound okra, cut into ¼-inch slices
oil for frying

1. Combine salt, flour, and cornmeal in a large bowl.
2. Add okra and toss until completely coated.
3. Have an adult heat 1 inch oil in a large skillet until hot. Do not allow oil to
   become so hot that it smokes.
4. Fry okra until crisp and golden.
5. Have an adult help you remove okra from oil.
6. Drain on paper towels before eating.

HISTORICAL TIMELINE

6,000 B.C.   Ancient people make Alabama their home.

A.D. 1540   Hernando de Soto attacks Choctaw Indians.

1711   Fort Louis de la Mobile becomes Alabama's first permanent European settlement.

1763   The French and Indian War ends, and France surrenders much of Alabama to Great Britain.

1783   After losing the American Revolution, Great Britain cedes Alabama and other land to Spain.

1814   Native Americans and U.S. troops fight the Battle of Horseshoe Bend against the Red Stick Creek.

1819   Alabama becomes the 22nd state.

1846   Montgomery becomes Alabama's state capital.

1861   Jefferson Davis is elected president of the Confederacy. Alabama withdraws from the United States.

1864 Union troops capture Mobile Bay.

1865 The Union wins the Civil War.

1881 Booker T. Washington founds the Tuskegee Normal and Industrial Institute.

1955 Rosa Parks is arrested in Montgomery for not yielding her seat to a white person.

1963 African Americans first attend the University of Alabama. George Wallace becomes governor of Alabama for the first time.

1965 Martin Luther King Jr. leads a march from Selma to Montgomery in protest against discriminatory voting restrictions.

1989 A memorial to honor people who died during the civil rights movement is built in Montgomery.

1993 Governor Guy Hunt is convicted of having misused public funds and is removed from office.

1995 Alabamian Heather Whitestone, who is hearing impaired, becomes the first Miss America with a disability.

2000 Voters in Alabama repeal the part of the state's constitution that banned marriage between whites and African Americans.

OUTSTANDING ALABAMIANS

Hank Aaron (born 1934), a retired baseball player from Mobile, was one of the best home-run hitters of all time. Aaron spent most of his career with the Milwaukee (later Atlanta) Braves. By 1974 he had hit 755 home runs, breaking Babe Ruth's all-time home-run record.

Hank Aaron

Tallulah Brockman Bankhead (1903–1968), born in Huntsville to a famous family of politicians, was an internationally known actress. She acted in theaters throughout London and New York, as well as in movies. Her performance in Alfred Hitchcock's movie *Lifeboat* won the New York Screen Critics' Award.

Tallulah Brockman Bankhead

Charles Barkley (born 1963), a basketball player, was born in Leeds. Barkley's career began when he was a star forward for Auburn University. Later, he played for the Philadelphia 76ers, the Phoenix Suns, and the Houston Rockets. He was a lead scorer for the gold medal-winning U.S. Olympic men's basketball teams in 1992 and 1996. Barkley retired from basketball in 2000.

Charles Barkley

Hugo Black (1886–1971) was a U.S. senator from Alabama for 10 years before becoming a U.S. Supreme Court judge in 1937. Black, from Harlan, strongly supported civil rights and free speech. He served on the court until his death.

W.E. Butterworth (born 1929) is the author of more than 100 books, many of them for children. Because he writes so much, Butterworth was named the Most Prolific Alabama Author of All Time in 1971. His books, many of which he writes under different pen names, include *LeRoy and the Old Man* and *Susan and Her Classic Convertible*. Butterworth lives in Fairhope, Alabama.

Hugo Black

George Washington Carver (1864?–1943), a scientist and educator, went to Alabama in 1896 to teach agriculture at Tuskegee Institute (later Tuskegee University). One of the institute's most famous instructors and researchers, Carver developed more than 300 products from peanuts, including powdered milk and soap.

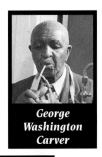

George Washington Carver

Mark Childress (born 1957) is a writer from Monroeville, Alabama. His novels include *A World Made of Fire* and *Crazy in Alabama*. Childress has also written *Joshua and Bigtooth*, a children's book.

Mark Childress

Nat "King" Cole (1917–1965) was a pianist and singer from Montgomery. His deep, mellow voice made him one of the most popular recording artists of the 1940s and 1950s. His many hits include "Straighten Up and Fly Right" and "Unforgettable."

Courteney Cox Arquette (born 1964) is an actress from Birmingham. She is known for her portrayal of Monica on the television series *Friends*. She also starred as Gale Weathers in the horror movies *Scream*, *Scream II*, and *Scream III*.

Nat "King" Cole

Emmylou Harris (born 1947) is a country-music singer, songwriter, and guitarist. Her best-known albums include *Luxury Liner*, *Blue Kentucky Girl*, and *Cowgirl's Prayer*. She has won several Grammy Awards and in 1980 was voted Female Vocalist of the Year by the Country Music Association. Harris is originally from Birmingham.

Mae C. Jemison (born 1956) is from Decatur, Alabama. In 1988 she became the first African American woman astronaut. In 1992 she was launched into orbit for the first time aboard the space shuttle *Endeavor*.

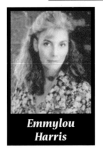

Emmylou Harris

Helen Keller

Coretta Scott King

Carl Lewis

Willie Mays

Helen Keller (1880–1968), from Tuscumbia, lost her sight and hearing when she was 19 months old. With the help of her teacher, Ann Sullivan, Keller learned to communicate and to read and write in Braille. Keller graduated with honors from Radcliffe College and devoted her life to improving conditions for the blind.

Coretta Scott King (born 1927), widow of civil rights leader Martin Luther King Jr., works to promote the rights of minorities, women, and the unemployed. King was born near Marion, Alabama.

Harper Lee (born 1926) won a Pulitzer Prize for her first and only novel, *To Kill a Mockingbird*, a young girl's account of her father defending a black man accused of a crime. The book has been translated into 10 languages. Lee is a native of Monroeville, Alabama.

Carl Lewis (born 1961) won four gold medals in track and field at the 1984 Olympic Games. He won medals in the 100-meter dash, the 200-meter dash, the long jump, and the 400-meter relay. Lewis is from Birmingham. Lewis also won gold in the 1988, 1992, and 1996 Olympics.

Willie Mays (born 1931), a native of Westfield, Alabama, was one of baseball's greatest athletes. Mays played center field for the New York (later San Francisco) Giants from 1951 until 1973. He was elected to the Baseball Hall of Fame in 1979.

Alexander McGillivray (1759?–1793), a leader of the Creek Indians, helped protect Creek land from white settlers by uniting the Creek and by signing treaties with the U.S. government. McGillivray was born near what later became Montgomery to a Scottish father and a half-French, half-Creek mother.

Jim Nabors (born 1932) played a goofy character named Gomer Pyle on *The Andy Griffith Show* and *Gomer Pyle, U.S.M.C.* He later hosted *The Jim Nabors Hour.* Born in Sylacauga, Alabama, Nabors is also an established singer, having recorded five gold albums.

Jim Nabors

Jesse Owens (1913–1980), a star track-and-field athlete, was born near Oakville, Alabama, and spent his childhood on a farm there. Owens won four gold medals at the 1936 Olympics in Berlin, Germany. In 1950 he was named Outstanding Track Athlete of the Half Century. Owens later traveled as a goodwill ambassador for the U.S. State Department.

Jesse Owens

Rosa Parks (born 1913) became a symbol for the civil rights movement when she refused to give up her seat on a bus to a white person. The bus driver had her arrested. This started large protests by blacks and whites across Alabama and the United States. Parks stood up for her belief that all people should be free and equal. She was born in Tuskegee, Alabama.

Waldo L. Semon (1898–1999), a chemist from Demopolis, Alabama, discovered polyvinyl chloride, also known as vinyl, in 1928. A type of plastic, vinyl is used in everything from clothing to cars.

Rosa Parks

Hank Williams Sr. (1923–1953) wrote and performed songs that made country music popular in regions other than the south and southwest. A singer and guitarist from Georgiana, Alabama, Williams composed more than 100 tunes, including "Hey, Good Lookin'" and "Your Cheatin' Heart."

Hank Williams

FACTS-AT-A-GLANCE

Nickname: Heart of Dixie

Song: "Alabama"

Motto: *Audemus Jura Nostra Defendere*
(We Dare Defend Our Rights)

Flower: camellia

Tree: southern longleaf pine

Bird: yellowhammer

Gemstone: star blue quartz

Insect: monarch butterfly

Nut: pecan

Reptile: Alabama red-bellied turtle

Date and ranking of statehood:
December 14, 1819, the 22nd state

Capital: Montgomery

Area: 50,750 square miles

Rank in area, nationwide: 28th

Average January temperature: 46° F

Average July temperature: 80° F

Alabama has changed its flag several times since it became a state in 1819. This design, modeled after the Confederate flag used during the Civil War, dates to 1895.

POPULATION GROWTH

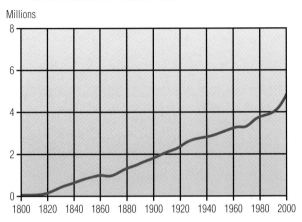

Millions

This chart shows how Alabama's population has grown from 1800 to 2000.

Alabama's state seal features a map of Alabama. On the map, rivers and borders are labeled. In 1819, when Alabama adopted the seal, rivers were the state's main routes for transporting goods and people.

Population: 4,447,100 (2000 census)

Rank in population, nationwide: 23rd

Major cities and populations: (2000 census) Birmingham (242,820), Montgomery (201,568), Mobile (198,915), Huntsville (158,216)

U.S. senators: 2

U.S. representatives: 7

Electoral votes: 9

Natural resources: coal, forests, limestone, natural gas, oil, rivers, soil

Agricultural products: beef cattle, chickens, corn, cotton, eggs, hay, hogs, milk, oats, peanuts, pecans, soybeans, wheat

Fishing industry: blue crabs, buffalo fish, catfish, mussels, oysters, shrimp

Manufactured goods: cement, chemicals, clothing, food products, paper products, steel

WHERE ALABAMIANS WORK

Service—56 percent (services includes jobs in trade; community, social, and personal services; finance, insurance, and real estate; transportation, communication, and utilities)

Manufacturing—17 percent

Government—16 percent

Construction—6 percent

Agriculture—4 percent

Mining—1 percent

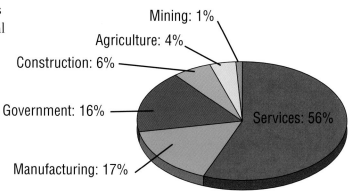

Mining: 1%
Agriculture: 4%
Construction: 6%
Government: 16%
Manufacturing: 17%
Services: 56%

GROSS STATE PRODUCT

Services—55 percent

Manufacturing—22 percent

Government—15 percent

Construction—4 percent

Agriculture—2 percent

Mining—2 percent

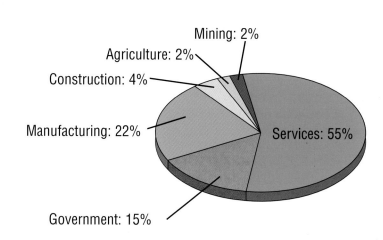

Mining: 2%
Agriculture: 2%
Construction: 4%
Manufacturing: 22%
Services: 55%
Government: 15%

ALABAMA WILDLIFE

Mammals: beaver, bobcat, deer, fox, mink, mouse, opossum, rabbit, raccoon, skunk, squirrel

Birds: ducks, geese, peregrine falcon, stork, turkey, woodpeckers

Reptiles and amphibians: turtle, alligator

Fish: bass, bream, buffalo fish, catfish, crappie, drumfish, flounder, garfish, mackerel, mullet, red snapper, shad, tarpon

Trees: cedar, cypress, hemlock, pine, oak

Wild plants: asters, azalea, Dutchman's-breeches, flowering dogwood, goldenrod, mountain laurel, orchids, pinks, rhododendron, southern camasses

Cottontail rabbit

Alligator

PLACES TO VISIT

Battleship Memorial Park, Mobile
Explore the USS *Alabama*, a World War II warship. Also at the park are vintage aircraft and the USS *Drum*, a submarine.

Birmingham Civil Rights Institute, Birmingham
Life in segregated Birmingham is depicted in exhibits, including a reconstruction of the separate schools attended by white and African American children. Racism, the civil rights movement, and international human rights are also explored.

Constitution Hall Village, Huntsville
This living history museum focuses on life in Alabama during the 1800s. The village commemorates Alabama's 1819 Constitutional Convention.

First White House of the Confederacy, Montgomery
A house museum in which visitors can explore the first capitol of the Confederacy. Viewers can also see artifacts from the life of Jefferson Davis, the Confederacy's president.

Fort Condé Museum and Welcome Center, Mobile
Costumed guides conduct tours of a reconstruction of a 1700s French fort. Visitors can learn about the history of Mobile up through the present day at the Welcome Center.

Horseshoe Bend National Military Park, Tallapoosa County
This 2,000-acre national military park marks the site of the 1814 Battle of Horseshoe Bend on the Tallapoosa River.

Moundville Archaeological Park

A 317-acre park surrounding earthworks created by Native Americans between 1000 and 1400. Visitors can tour a recreated temple and more than 20 mounds. Artifacts are on display at the Jones Archaeological Museum.

Russell Cave National Monument, near Bridgeport

This archaeological site contains artifacts and signs of human habitation almost 10,000 years ago. Park rangers conduct tours of the cave, and visitors can explore a museum.

Tuskegee Institute

Visitors can see original structures—built by Tuskegee students using hand-made bricks—in the Historic Campus District. The on-campus National Historic Site explores African American history, industrialization, and the legacy of Booker T. Washington and George Washington Carver.

U.S. Army Aviation Museum, Fort Rucker

This museum houses one of the world's largest collections of helicopters. Displays trace the U.S. Army's aviation from its first helicopter, the R-4, to the newest choppers.

U.S. Space and Rocket Center, Huntsville

Artifacts including moon rocks and spacecraft displays in Rocket Park draw visitors to this site. Explorers can ride in machines that simulate space flight, such Mars Mission, which takes riders on a "trip" across the planet Mars.

ANNUAL EVENTS

Mardi Gras, Mobile—*February–March*

Southeastern Livestock Exposition Rodeo and Livestock Week, Montgomery—*March*

Catfish Festival, Ariton—*April*

Birmingham International Festival, Birmingham—*April*

Chilton County Peach Festival, Clanton—*June*

W.C. Handy Music Festival, Florence—*August*

Jackson County Fair, Scottsboro—*September*

Moundville Native American Festival, Moundville—*October*

National Shrimp Festival, Gulf Shores—*October*

National Peanut Festival, Dothan—*November*

Holiday Festival, Selma—*December*

LEARN MORE ABOUT ALABAMA

General

Davis, Lucile. *Alabama.* Chicago: Children's Press, 1999. For older readers.

Fradin, Dennis Brindell. *Alabama.* Chicago: Children's Press, 1995.

Wills, Charles. *A Historical Album of Alabama.* Brookfield, CT: The Millbrook Press, 1995.

Special Interest

Amper, Thomas. *Booker T. Washington.* Minneapolis, MN: Carolrhoda Books, Inc., 1998. This easy reader focuses on Washington's struggle to get an education.

Mitchell, Barbara. *A Pocketful of Goobers.* Minneapolis, MN: Carolrhoda Books, Inc., 1986. George Washington Carver's work with peanuts and Alabama farmers is the focus of this biography.

Parks, Rosa. *I Am Rosa Parks.* New York: Dial Books for Young Readers, 1997. The life story of civil rights activist Rosa Parks, a native of Alabama, who refused to give her seat on a bus up to a white man. Rosa Parks's action is often cited as the first event of the civil rights movement.

Stein, Richard Conrad. *The Montgomery Bus Boycott.* Chicago: Children's Press, 1994. An exploration of the Montgomery bus boycott of 1955–1956.

Fiction

Banks, Sarah Harrall. *Under the Shadow of Wings.* New York: Atheneum Books for Young Readers, 1997. Eleven-year-old Tattnall tries to help her brain-damaged cousin in World War II-era rural Alabama.

Capote, Truman. *A Christmas Memory.* New York: Alfred A. Knopf, 1997. A 1930s Christmas in rural Alabama as seen through the eyes of seven-year-old Buddy. Aunt Sook and Buddy celebrate the season and their special bond. For older readers.

Johnson, Angela. *The Other Side.* New York: Orchard Books, 1998. A book of poems that recall the African American author's girlhood in Alabama. Photographs of the author illustrate the poems.

Lee, Harper. *To Kill a Mockingbird.* New York: HarperCollins, 1999. For older readers. This 1960 Pulitzer Prize-winning novel tells the story of two children, their lawyer father, and a man unjustly accused of a terrible crime.

McKissak, Patricia. *Run Away Home.* New York: Scholastic Books, 1997. In 1888 a girl with an African American father and a Native American mother helps an Apache boy hide after he escapes a train bound for a reservation.

WEBSITES

AlaWeb
<http://www.state.al.us/>
The state of Alabama's official website. Find facts about state government, tourism, and history.

Alabama Bureau of Tourism and Travel
<http://www.touralabama.org/>
Visitors to Alabama can plan trips in the state using this website, featuring events and other Alabama-related information.

Alabama Department of Archives and History
<http://www.archives.state.al.us>
Provides extensive Internet access to information about Alabama's history. A kids page and links to other cites are provided.

Birmingham Post-Herald
<http://www.postherald.com/>
A daily newspaper's website that focuses on news and events in the Birmingham area.

Montgomery Advertiser
<http://www.montgomeryadvertiser.com/>
This daily newspaper's website provides information about news and events in Montgomery.

PRONUNCIATION GUIDE

Chattahoochee (chat-uh-HOO-chee)

Cheaha (CHEE-haw)

Cherokee (CHEHR-uh-kee)

Chickasaw (CHIHK-uh-saw)

Choctaw (CHAHK-taw)

Dauphin (DAW-fuhn)

Le Moyne, Pierre and Jean Baptiste
(luh-mwahn, pee-YEHR and
zhawn bah-TEEST)

Muskogean (muhs-KOH-gee-uhn)

Sequoyah (sih-KWOY-uh)

Tecumseh (tuh-KUHMP-suh)

Tombigbee (tahm-BIHG-bee)

Tuskegee (tuhs-KEE-gee)

At the Marshall Space Flight Center in Huntsville, Alabama, an astronaut practices making repairs in an underwater facility.

GLOSSARY

carpetbagger: a term used by Southerners to describe Northerners who came to the South after the Civil War to make money. The name carpetbagger suggests that Northerners carried everything they owned in a carpetbag, or suitcase.

civil rights movement: a movement to gain equal rights, or freedoms, for all citizens—regardless of race, religion, and sex

colony: a territory ruled by a country some distance away

lock: an enclosed water-filled chamber in a canal or river used to raise or lower boats beyond the site of a waterfall

plantation: a large estate, usually in a warm climate, on which crops are grown by workers who live on the estate. In the past, plantation owners usually used slave labor.

precipitation: rain, snow, and other forms of moisture that fall to earth

Reconstruction: the period from 1865 to 1877, during which the U.S. government brought the Southern states back into the Union after the Civil War. Before rejoining the Union, a Southern state had to pass a law allowing black men to vote. Places destroyed in the war were rebuilt, and industries were developed.

reservoir: a place where water is collected and stored for later use

swamp: a wetland permanently soaked with water. Woody plants (trees and shrubs) are the main forms of vegetation.

INDEX

PHOTO ACKNOWLEDGMENTS

Cover (left): © Philip Gould/CORBIS; Cover (right): © Lowell Georgia/CORBIS; © Richard A. Cooke/CORBIS, pp.2–3; © Richard Cummins/CORBIS, p. 3; © Mary A. Root/Root Resources, pp. 4, 7, 16, 17, 40, 53; Johnny Autery, pp. 6, 10, 14; William H. Allen, Jr., pp. 11, 12, 41, 42, 46, 73; Jean Higgins, p. 13; © Steve Kaufman/CORBIS, pp. 15; Library of Congress, pp. 18, 20, 26, 29, 34, 66 (bottom); Museums of the City of Mobile, pp. 19, 22; IPS, p. 21; © Bettmann/CORBIS, pp. 24, 69 (second from top); Smithsonian Institution, p. 25; AmSouth Bank, p. 27; University of South Alabama Archives: Erik Overbey Collection, p. 30; Minneapolis Public Library, p. 31; Addsco Collection, p. 33; Archives Collection, Birmingham Public Library, Birmingham, AL, p. 35; UPI/Bettmann/CORBIS, p. 36; Alabama Dept. of Archives and History, p. 37; NE Stock Photo: Jim Schwabel, pp. 38, 54, 60; Robert Boyer, pp. 43, 53; Barbara Laatsch-Hupp/Laatsch-Hupp Photo, p. 44; © Raymond Gehman/CORBIS, pp. 47, 48; Frederica Georgia, p. 49; © Richard T. Nowitz/CORBIS, p. 50; University of Alabama, p. 51; Alabama Bureau of Tourism and Travel, p. 52; Bill Lea, p. 56; James A. Deason II, p. 57; Alabama Forestry Commission, pp. 58, 59; Atlanta Braves, p. 66 (top); © Hutton-Deutsch Collection/CORBIS, p. 66 (second from top); © AFP/CORBIS, p. 66 (second from bottom); USDA, p. 67 (top); Jerry Bauer/G. P. Putnam's Sons, p. 67 (second from top); TV Times, p. 67 (second from bottom); Caroline Greyshock, p. 67 (bottom); Dictionary of American Portraits, p. 68 (top); © David & Peter Tumley/CORBIS, p. 68 (second from top); University of Houston, p. 68 (second from bottom); San Francisco Giants, p. 68 (bottom); Hollywood Book & Poster Co., p. 69 (top, bottom); Schomberg Center for Research in Black Culture, the New York Public Library, Astor, Lenox, and Tilden, p. 69 (second from bottom); Jean Matheny, p. 70; Lynn M. Stone, p. 73 (bottom); © Roger Ressmeyer/CORBIS, p. 80.